WE ARE
HOPELESSLY
SMALL AND
MODERN BIRDS

WE ARE
HOPELESSLY
SMALL AND
MODERN BIRDS

SARA LEFSYK

Black
Lawrence
Press

Black
Lawrence
Press

www.blacklawrence.com

Executive Editor: Diane Goettel
Book and Cover Design: Amy Freels

Copyright © 2017 Sara Lefsyk
ISBN: 978-1-62557-997-3

Published 2018 by Black Lawrence Press.
Printed in the United States.

CONTENTS

For and After Federico García Lorca   I

Section//1

As If A Man Splits   5
Take, For Instance, A Planet   6
It's Impossible To Reach My Tiny Body   7
Last Night I Dreamt   8
All My Life I've Been Dragging   9
Occasionally, Our Apartment Complex   10
This Is Agony   11
I'm Tired Of These Sorts of Walls   12
In The Event That We Are, After All   13

Section//2

I Had This Friend   17
If It Takes Time   18
It Was A Day   19
They Made Blindfolds   20
The Company Of The Day Of Fish   21
If They Were Counting   22
I Was Out Way Out   23
Heidegger Was Doing His Feelings   24
Heidegger Touches My Ocean   25
If I Were A Wife   26
I'm Alive In The Tiny Colony   27

Section//3

It will take me twenty paces   31

"I can't speak in sounds"   32

I don't think I can take credit for this   33

I had been killing the strange arms   34

I am sleepwalking with William James   35

What we did with the old pins   36

We're at the actual museum   37

I am in the next room   38

Section//4

Once, I met a man who could divide himself   41

No one knows if I grew out of bees   42

Murdered in the prayer room at night   43

At night, we make the sounds animals make   44

We didn't have a chance to do a
     classical strange situation sequence   45

That night, we slept perilously close to the animal   46

Today we can preserve out behavior   47

I had fainted in the fixed muteness of sparrows   48

Then we fought about whether to
     encounter the animals   49

Section//5

A small man looked at me   53

I told this small man   54

Then a small man looked at me   55

Oh! I says to a small man   56

We were sitting in the space   57

A small man looked straight at me   58

This is the basic principal   59

One night I dreamt   60
On another day, a small man says to me   61
I have wrapped myself   62
At this point, a man and I   63

for and after FEDERICO GARCÍA LORCA

It was the hour of sleeping crocodiles. Federico, you tossed a wilderness of bleeding pigeons into my heart. I said: take me to the friend of dead-smashed butterflies. Take me to the miniature priests of idiot-brains.

And Federico, you climbed the great mountain of burnt-up flowers in the dark saying: "One must wait a thousand years under the cancerous moon to touch the dried-out body of the moth.

And because blood has no sadness, one must drown her gods in a sea of infinite kitchens."

Federico! Seller of the sky and of gutted-out horses, of the lost landscape of the apple, and the eyes of dogs and skulls and of dug-up roots. You wore a night-mask of phosphorous and sharp lilies and tore the hem of my gown.

And I said, Federico of a million granite buildings and of tears, I want a strand that will tremble in the presence of your stillness. But it was the moment of live fish and broken microscopes and you lifted the black curtains of air. Your face a bud of light, you smashed the mute fossil of living air and gave to me an earring and handfuls of rope.

But I wanted to sleep the sleep of the infinite crocodile inside your golden chest, so I tied eight ghosts and a thousand sequins to your hair and wore the gloves of one hundred sadnesses under the lemon shadow of your actual dreams.

Federico of torn cloth and murdered grass, of the terrible violence of ants and the nocturnal rooster of madness. Federico of a thousand tiny birds.

I//

AS IF A MAN SPLITS into a very old bone and dwells in it, and when he passes that bone's shadow it's like nothing-else. Then he goes to his plate and draws pictures of bitten words.

And we clearly like this way of doing things.

Still, we could go days without being in our bodies and then a little man would come naked and take us up to his fifth-floor apartment and feed us pharmacological pancakes.

Those were the days before the asylum, when we sheltered ourselves with floorboards, and I dreamt I was floating through Kentucky, and all my birds were as unrecognizable as the kitchen sink.

You were all burning yourselves on the outskirts of some town, feeling very alone, and quoting the greatest historical figures of our time.

I saw an industrial landscape and reenacted a scene from my early childhood disembodiment: imagine a municipal airport, an old-fashioned bird, and technology.

That was the year we were so haunted we couldn't even look at a modern building without hallucinating bathroom mirrors.

It was fine though, to live that way.

TAKE, FOR INSTANCE, A PLANET. We motioned like the eyes of dead animals in stairwells that weren't yet submerged in the corners of ants.

We were in some strange plaza full of the fish-of-what-didn't-hurt-for-once-in-our-lives and the light that came through all its many coats was a bit like the greatest season of the framework of all parenting of all time that we could remember that ever existed.

All my fingers were insecure patients in both the National Public Hospital of Kentucky and the Kingdom of Fecundity-Gowns. Still, the moon passes over some façades and even the darkest places grow machine-like in our altitude.

What we want is to roll around in the overall zones, Messiah, we said, then placed our hands inside our mouths

and swallowed.

IT'S IMPOSSIBLE TO REACH MY TINY BODY in the hospital in time for them to understand that i made most of this up in a dream. It's 2:30 in the morning and people extend backwards and forwards in time in every direction.

Meanwhile, the Socialist Party rents a room in my building that forms a sort-of staircase over Kant's bathroom, while Kant's bathroom forms a sort-of storehouse in which i keep my psychology bags and my actual potential space.

At 6 in the morning Kant flushes the toilet and my feet barely reach the ground.

Outside my window, the Socialist Party is having a bake sale, and I search all my drawers for all the medications they ever gave me so that, when the Messiah comes, we may all eat cookies and take pills

and that's the basic miracle.

LAST NIGHT I DREAMT I was an intricate barricade in the house of a flying bird. Kant was a ferocious glass skylark and all the little golden lemons were hanging over our heads.

But the Messiah was false as were the tablecloths.

And it didn't take a genius to figure that Kant knew only the love of kitchen utensils and sheet music because, when a beautiful woman walked by, "I understand the loneliness of a creator among beehives," is all he ever said.

And because all of life happens under her dress, I took mine off and asked Kant to read the astronomy of my pelvis. But he couldn't find one word in him, only a paper doll which he pulled from his pocket and offered over to me.

On some other nights, an old man sleeps beside me, but only in his dreams, so that when we wake we no longer have the ceiling above nor the floor beneath.

Meanwhile, the Socialist Party is carving the likeness of various astronomical distances out of the walls, ceilings and floorboards.

ALL MY LIFE I'VE BEEN DRAGGING up other people's beds and fixing my body against the world.

In my shadow the alphabet takes the form of a classroom in which the Messiah is an unlikely animal sniffing the edges of this page.

We broke the law variously then retreated to our holy spheres where thousands of roosters sway in the darkness like violins.

Which is wider: a distant picture of my mother or the way my drunk father breathes his oxygen?

A man is walking through a wooden staircase as if his whole body is only the reflection of his other body, which contains the reflection of a rooster swaying in the dark holy realms of a contemporary wind.

If we go out into the fields, Kentucky will eat our bodies whole and spread them across the atmosphere like so many dead fish. If we throw a stone into the air, it'll bounce off our face and form a sort-of wild core

because for a very long time we have been staring into the eyes of these dolls.

OCCASIONALLY, OUR APARTMENT COMPLEX floats out to sea. As it was, Kant and I had our noses somewhere in the distance. "Most likely there is no meaning in things," Kant says. "Or only in the ultimate logic of certain animal forms and avian noises."

For this reason my bones feel like the small broken bones of a very tiny goldfish.

This is the basic tragedy: for as long as I can remember we have been peeling layers off the interior walls of the Interior Ministry and within each layer various heavenly bodies have grown old and died.

What does this sound like?

Below us the Socialist Party is painting murals on the ocean's water from which point one can view a valley and certain regions of space.

THIS IS AGONY: beneath America there is another more American America. There is a strange sky created by multiple age-old functional systems and even the suicidal eyes of miniature birds say: *nothing is ancient anymore anyway.*

There is no hidden mouth the whiteness of fields holds vigil over.

Of all things I buried my windows and all the snapshots of a man taking snapshots of me burying my windows.

Who's going to build my mind a modern-day kitchen?

Whose going to loan me legroom in the National Public Hospital of Kentucky? Because the water that is in us is very psychological and sometimes seems like another whole person altogether.

Sometimes our bodies become very historical.

At the old train yard, Kant's body stands on air and I run my fingers over his face then mine to compare the different ways we're each asleep.

"When the Messiah comes," Kant says, "let's invite him over to my place and medicate our roosters, then fly them up to the National Public Archives and buy ourselves some realnice sweaters.

I'M TIRED OF THESE SORTS OF WALLS never being quite big enough to see through. Or if only they were transparent and we could thread our bodies to some sort of International Museum of Sleep Deprivation. Or surface walking. Or both.

Then maybe we could skip eviction and take up malaria as a hobby. Here. In this house.

But the Socialists have been preparing for this for thousands of years and so Kant has emptied his apartment and I have taken my pigeons out into the streets to snack on various sorts of breads and cheeses.

And because I am terrified of certain types of art and kitchens and Kant has a momentary hunger for hallucinogens and wild carp, we ride our bicycles out to the National Public Pharmacies

behind the river but in front of the sea.

From this place we can feel our bodies pass through a banknote: "and so maybe," Kant says: "we have been digging holes and lying beside them this whole time after all."

Indeed, we could compose *A Book of Serious Medications* and live off it for weeks!

IN THE EVENT THAT WE ARE, AFTER ALL, only giant holographic images of one another, Kant and I reach into the cloud chamber to get a realtrue sense of things.

And while I have devoted my life to writing my master's thesis on the transcription of bird shapes and animal voices, Kant rolls out his projector and screen and swims for hours in a film of the sea.

When we describe what it's like to see what we have seen we say: *when you invent things like light you really do suffer*

and: *I'm afraid the height of your eyes will expand in my abdomen and cause all the little birds buried there to decompose before their time.*

This one thing is necessary.

Throughout the day my body becomes a millennium of seagulls and seashit and it's as if I had spent the whole night in the arms of some deadman and for this reason I can't understand how there is so much solitude in Kant's fingers and why his veins carry him so much as if through an insomnia of underground tunnels and cabins.

In the morning, we abandon our footsteps and the southernmost point of this goddamned earth is such a circling in my eyes that Kant must cover his ears as I become astronomical in distance.

Above us, the Socialist Party is laying tin cans over the roof so that, when the bigbig rain comes, we may all sleep imprisoned somewhere between the landscape of the rooster and the landscape of the sea.

2//

I HAD THIS FRIEND who was a medium. Heidegger concludes: "here is the bleak city of Rochester"

then he descends all on me. But my body is nowhere and we wake to something we have really only read about in dreams.

Oh, how the cleaning lady has stroked his back and carried my fist! Therefore, how do I say *no* when she begs for water?

These are secret thoughts.

Someone found the dentist in her apartment and the beloved, he descends all on me in the manner of a headache and a poor memory.

What would a mother think? I lost my t-shirt in the prayer closet then thanked the son for his time.

IF IT TAKES TIME you probably want to see this: the son rocked me shut in the church then pulled the underwear from my body.

My body was everywhere.

You want to wonder about ropes but it's important to stay still and let the son gain everything.

All my sisters crowded the dr. then let him have his way. But my body was an apron and the son wore it like it mattered.

That was his brilliance. Under the eaves of the hospital.

That was our brilliance.

IT WAS A DAY like any other day like no other. That being said, the dr. himself confiscated my pills.

Who's to say?!

Your dr. does trip regularly on aspirin tablets but the logic of the fish remains indescribable.

If it takes time it's probably not worth doing.

THEY MADE BLINDFOLDS of our eyes but we went transparent anyway. Sometimes, in the cathedral, over and over, we are made to lose what's pure. Still, the pharmacist practices good penmanship and all my sisters bite their vegetables like they mean it.

I refuse to believe I can't sell maps to the cartographer.

All I want is for the cartographer to touch my body and heal it. But the son continuously puts his hands over my mouth and eyes and tells me not to move.

THE COMPANY OF THE DAY OF FISH is going. Still, the husband was a good man. I can't say enough about my propensity for his brand existed.

Among the names of my regions there was something of a distance. I could sing my mother but still she would not feed me.

The son came up to my pelvis and threw his elbow: "We have to kill what is in you!"

I simply can't say enough about my propensity for the son. All the dr.'s patients wear lipstick and faint real money.

Among the names of the husband I walk beside him. They found my underwear in his parking lot.

Oh, what a good man.

IF THEY WERE COUNTING us all they were counting us all like they did yesterday only this time they would miss me in the numbers today.

Then they would force us onto our feet and we would pray for there not to be ropes and if there were ropes we would pray.

Arrange yourself.

The dr. himself would kneel before us and stick things places i can't even talk about

and we won't even cry a little after all.

They found my t-shirt but not me in it in the prayer room. They found my silence and my t-shirt and i did pray.

Bless me, they found my whole body in some dentist's apartment and rotated it until they found its brilliance.

My upper jaw fit into my pelvis and i became some good factory.

I WAS OUT WAY OUT past my bedtime. Heidegger swore he didn't sell my cash. He said: "I go into and out of this supermarket whenever I want," then tossed the fish onto the planes.

Someone has to tear my body from its body.

The surgeon took me to the amphitheater then rubbed my parts. This made absolutely no difference.

When his eyes are closed and no one is looking, Heidegger's caseworker touches my breast and says I'm some good factory.

I like it best in the cathedral when we fill my body with nitrogen. I like this sort of nitrogen when we fill my body with cathedral and my body is nowhere.

I like it when the dr. takes his time with me, but the son has philosophical hands and all I want is to draw circles around his footsteps.

HEIDEGGER WAS DOING HIS FEELINGS-through-the-wall thing, I could see him, let-me-tell-you! "I know this earth rotates." I remember his voice like a slow-motion film.

I remember the discount pill pharmacy.

All I wanted was a gyroscope in my peripheral. The son took me to the industrial park then touched my parts. My dress was a torrent anyone's sister will tell you.

No one lives anywhere for free.

I took up my weapons and called it an afternoon. Under the eaves of the hospital the son took my precious precious then dragged me through the fresh fruit market.

All I wanted was for the cartographer to scratch my veins. I like it best in the cathedral when we fill my body with nitrogen. Like this we entered many summers as intellectuals.

But my sisters all jumped the circuit and hit up mad Republicans. All I want is for a humming sound and to have an international virus.

HEIDEGGER TOUCHES MY OCEAN with his voice: "I put the bill in yr name." But I only have a small amount of ether and the dr. x-rays my uterus until I bleed out.

Still, the son puts his fingers all up in me and tries to pull out what's his.

It's important to let the son gain everything.

I try to explain that I don't have a nervous disorder but dr. continuously fills my veins with yellow liquid until I pass out and come to again.

"One can never be too sure."

Part of my body is in vain and the other part is everywhere. If I say "I put the bill in yr name," I mean I walked through the ether and came out floating in a slow-motion film.

IF I WERE A WIFE and a mother I
would be a wife and a mother. All my
children say: "Build me," but the son
takes my pelvis and runs it through the
supermarket.

I go into and out of this supermarket
whenever I want.

And because letters form my name, the
dr. releases me onto my raft endlessly.
Heidegger sheds his pennies into my
ocean but my sisters all take up arms

and our bodies are really only something
we have read about in dreams.

"Insanity is a word reminiscent of your
eyes," says the son. Then he slaps my face
as if I were his wife

or his mother.

**I'M ALIVE IN THE TINY
COLONY** of sisters but I refuse to wake
up among them. I refuse language and
bite the dr.'s fingers repeatedly. I bite his
lip and, because they found my
brilliance in some dentist's apartment, I
open the drawers of my body.

Heidegger kneels over me and, because I
am everywhere, he takes my sternum
and writes his sermon over it.

The son has dowsing rods and all my
sisters are hungry, but the angles of the
planets mean nothing is worth
happening.

Heidegger swoons impossibly, a fish
over the planes, and it's not even Sabbath
but the dr. takes our light bulbs and
makes us stare into the dark endlessly.

3//

IT WILL TAKE ME TWENTY PACES to get to that tree. Meanwhile, William James is boxing somewhere in the corner. I can see his pony from here. I say: next climb onto that bridge and wait there, William. At night some things can reappear.

Like the time they told me to make a doll out of clock parts but instead I made a strobe light and sat on it for a while.

The whole scene went something like this: a man, seeing a transparent dog walk on air, walks off the edge of a hill and falls into his world alone. He says: "My hand is red and on fire. We are using someone else's night voices."

At night a woman wears blue and forgets about weather.

In this next scene William is trying to convince me to build a clock out of doll parts. When I say: I want to trick William into the very air, I mean: I need a benefactor the size of his ghost. I water his birds but still he will not let go of cloth and lend me his gown.

"I CAN'T SPEAK IN SOUNDS," says a man. We are at the old speakeasy pounding clay. It's morning. If I make a brief picture of a very modern horse, William makes bird musculature. If I make the first short gown of night, William drags me deep into the field and tells me: "Sally, it is vital that you do not look up."

But I can't facilitate the apparitions, William, I say. And how do you facilitate all these apparitions?

When William can't answer I have no way to tell if I am ok. When he drops all his dolls over the breakwater, there is a sort-of animal-shape hovering above.

I DON'T THINK I CAN TAKE CREDIT FOR THIS: the whole house was in pain but we went to the market anyway to spend our dimes. At the old fish breeder's William recalls how, in his youth, he had been haunted by trout in the Great Bering Sea.

But a man is a doll made out of tiny bird parts. "There is a sort-of animal-shape hovering above," he says. William says, "What!" then eats a very tiny salted cracker. His whole second body expands inside his first. "All is well inside the first and second bodies," he explains, "the world held together with rope, various beams and rope."

Still, a woman wakes up and feels a wilderness. She says, "I feel the wilderness moving inside of me moving outside of me."

It's dark.

A man is listening to other people's animal voices.

"William's pony is red and on fire" he says. Then places whelk in his ears and collapses to the floor of his inner visions.

I HAD BEEN KILLING THE STRANGE ARMS of my soul when William came up from this animal. "I am absolutely a scientist!" he was shouting. "If I am going to live in any city in America then I am absolutely a scientist!"

But a man sat crying with small birds in his face, "I must fashion myself a gown of high water." Then took his face down to the river to untie it to the river.

We are at the height of a great mountain wading in our own gutters of brightbright stars. William says it is the year of the goat or something, but a man sits dreaming the darkest dreams of moths, forgetting the names and colors of things.

And although one hundred tiny birds could fit inside his form, he is eight times any river.

"Whatever the river does I will do," William tells a man to say. But a woman is running with plates. She has knives in her arms and cannot feel her body. "Any animal is an ocean at night," she says. Then lies down and goes comatose in the river.

I AM SLEEPWALKING WITH WILLIAM JAMES
and his pony, toward the wall that forms his dress, when William goes shouting about silence down the darkwet streets.

With what will one day be a bird in his brain, he asks, "Does it bother you when I shout this way, LIKE THIS?!"

No, I say, only it's painful, like growing bones here around a spirit.

William says that suffering is something we should do a little of everyday. But I am wearing the mask of a chicken over a mask of a man and still I cannot tell the stars from other peoples' faces.

"And because we are a drunkards in a city of thieves," William explains, "we are supposed to know magic and eat it for them."

WHAT WE DID WITH THE OLD PINS was
unmistakable, nine animals remained but only one was still
alive.

We're at the old Jungian Theatre touching walls. I want to
build a trout out of bird parts but William wears a girl's ugly
face and says his orange juice tastes like potatoes

and can you make orange juice out of potatoes?

I tell William no, I cannot make orange juice out of tomatoes.
I am wearing my Gettysburg hat. It's winter. The snow forms
a sort-of doorway into the ground.

With any effort a man's face is a bud of light

when he's floating and at sea. In a deserted plaza, his face is
an academy of pure holes and plaster. He says: "I don't believe
in a secret-real self. But it's far too dangerous."

A woman wakes up thinking violent.

Her fingers move toward the dead eyes of a bird. She says she
feels the animals moving outside of her moving inside of her.

A film plays on screen. It's a fast-motion action-documentary
containing a close-up of the world and a still frame of a very
modern-day pony.

WE'RE AT THE ACTUAL MUSEUM of modern day history, realigning ourselves with the great spectral figures of our time. William wears the dress of altered states and explains how: "*Church* is a roundabout way of saying *lunch* or *biscuits*," then puts on a type of coat.

Still, a man sits learning the names and colors of things. He no longer believes in the mind of a bird. This is his dharma: he points at the clear sky endlessly when a woman is breaking heliotropes in half. "I have almost fainted to be in commercials," she says, then runs out to the terrible mass of actual trees.

She is a hill upon a hill if she is a mountain. She is a slow-motion picture star. "I really feel it is as if there were birds" she says, then lies down in the grass or in the aperture.

When William is deconstructing the mind of a bird, he is interpreting the animal exegesis. "If it weren't for the hive of my being I'd think like animals think," he says.

When he refuses his dharma, he is recalling the hard land of his youth, where once he ate cereal with a real man for ten hours. "Real men never point at the clear sky and say 'real sky'

endlessly."

I AM IN THE NEXT ROOM when the deer comes through William. When it spreads its fast-blue fur a woman sits up and touches weather. "Who's going to stoke my diagnosis?" she asks.

But William's stars are falling all over our buildings and *can you please stop them for a minute?* we beg. "The world is a brilliant hospital and man's face is thus accurate," William replies, all naked-like and almost-wild.

Throughout winter William remains gorgeously riven in some other world. Searching for the perfect zero, he kisses small animals between cold air. "This is my dharma," he explains, then stretches out beneath the geometric star-like hides of horses.

He is a hopelessly small and modern bird. He has a thousand rivers inside and a thousand rivers inside each of those.

411

Once, I met a man who could divide himself into lakes. "It is imminent," he said, "we are aligning ourselves with the great spectral figures of our time."

Then, with a landscape of pheasants in his eyes, and the darkness of hospitals in my blood, we spilled a thousand empty moons.

We had to.

No one knows if I grew out of bees or out of horses. A needle is at the center of the bees or a knife and birds sink continuously out into my channels.

Then a Savior comes falling out of my dreams.

He is wearing birds or birds sleep in his hair at night. "To make things with our hands means to make things with our hands," he says, "and I need more lengths of rope.

Because to be tender is to have the face of the sky, but to be unafraid is to have the face of everything."

Murdered in the prayer room at night with birds dreaming in my head. My fear is that they will get stuck in here or that I can't pray them out.

Then a Savior comes lashing himself to me at night. "We are susceptible to many birds dreaming in our heads," he says.

But my stable-mate wakes with her mouth full of moths. Or she injects herself with deities and then weeps like one.

And a man has the sad eyes of a fish in an empty plaza full of wounded birds. And he bows to the anarchy of his infinite failures.

Because once these birds fall out of our heads, we can no longer feel the animals come bite us.

At night, we make the sounds animals make. Not against the sky, but perfect and good.

Once we have followed the animals into the trees, then we have clearly made miracles happen.

Because if we have walked through the trees and survived the animals, we may take up alms as we have taken up knives.

We didn't have a chance to do a classical strange situation sequence because of the frequent occurrences of animal magnetism.

But my stable-mate is drunk on the stem and grinds her teeth into the sidewalk until only the eternal cloud remains.

And a man weeps at the feet of a saint. And the animals glisten before they're devoured by sleep.

That night, we slept perilously close to the animal. I woke with my dress falling through its hands.

Savior took my name and gave it to the animal: If-I-want-a-clean-house-I-have- to-do-it-myself.

"There are seven windows given to animals." He told me to make an eighth.

Today, we can preserve our behavior by hearing instead of feeling the floating feeling. Instead of hearing.

Birds do that.
They have to.

But the animals together run from the sky or rise from close to the ground. And either we taste the animals or the animals taste us, then spill the moon into our thousand empty faces

and tie our fingers against the worm. In the hours after the hour of mud.

I had fainted in the fixed muteness of sparrows, but a man stood above the ashes of dead fish.

He said he saw the light float past on minute ships. And because the animals had weakened on sulphur, and their edges were widening, we were tying their faces against cold air.

Lifting pieces of sulphur with air, standing on high chairs and crying. Biting our teeth into the animal.

We had to.

Then we fought about whether to encounter the animals with our hands, or to just brush them into the water.

And we could feel the animal parts of ourselves, or we hovered above them watching.

No one knows.

5//

A SMALL MAN LOOKED AT ME. He said "You are the Fritz Perls look-alike in the apartment complex of my life and I want to make a tincture out of your saline eye drops and ride away with you into the desert in a Cadillac full of very small and miniature ponies."

I TOLD THIS SMALL MAN: if I had a mule, a parachute and long, flowing locks, I would jump out of this plane, put you in my shopping cart and push you to Brazil where we would change our names, cut our hair, and join the local militia. After that, we would lead a small army of chickens to the sea and, after many days of floating, I would catch a small fish and name it Pavlov. Then we would all jump into the sea and swim until we reached the largest island in Europe, where we would start a mariachi band with my birth family and yours and the sun would set and we would all drink sugar water and go to sleep beneath a large curtain of black air.

THEN A SMALL MAN LOOKED AT ME. He said, "If I had a boat and a boating license I would sail you through this desert to a place where they produce real-nice-life-size-kitten-knick-knacks and I would buy you one. After several days we would walk to the local barber, each wearing the mask of a chicken over the mask of a man. While there, we would get our hair styled in braids weaved from the beard hair of eight male ghosts and sequins and then we would wander out to the-place-where-trees-grow and stay there with the trees dreaming of our various departed pets until we didn't want to stay there any longer. And then we would go someplace else, I-don't-even-know-where."

OH! I SAYS TO A SMALL MAN, I had not yet been born but I knew someday I would wear a ruffle gown and whore's makeup. And still, after all these years, it feels as if I am not born and no matter what shoes I wear I still cannot get my feet to touch the ground. It is as if I am Mark Epstein's patient and he keeps trying to get me to wear his clothes. Maybe if I just put on a pair of his pants and a tie he will teach me the art of fiddle-carving.

All I ever wanted was to fiddle in a hardcore band.

WE WERE SITTING IN THE SPACE between the spider and the space between the bed when a small man looked at me. He said his head hurt so he went out to lay down in the waves, which were actually multitudes of tiny homeostatic sequins tied together with the beard hair of eight male ghosts. He said he heard we could become fishers of men, but we decided we had better things to do, and I never wanted to become a night nurse anyway. The small man said he had always doubted the reality of symbolism in modern art. Because of this, his claim was that we all had become far too preoccupied with the industrialization of contemporary furniture. And as he had spoken directly with Vladimir Nabokov in a dream the night before, he was certain that each man was a structure made only of empty rooms full of narcissism pathologies. Then we put on our whale-shaped backpacks and travelled somewhere we could pitch camp for the night and celebrate Passover properly.

A SMALL MAN LOOKED STRAIGHT AT ME, shouting, "If you do not behave I will never take you to see a resurrection ever again! As it is I feel really terrible about the way I forced you to pitch camp for the night and fix all the dressings, and it's all I can do to not gather twelve men to women and travel out into the wilderness where we would use your guts as a tightrope to cross the canyon and lasso many wild horses, which we would ride right into a mighty snowbank. In this sort-of new world economy that would form out of the snowbank, we would both form and join a Yiddish army, living out the rest of our lives in bunny sleepers of sorts. But ones that button up, not zip. And they have little beads stitched into them. And they are made out of such nice fabric all anyone would want to do is touch them.

BUT THEY CAN'T!"

THIS IS THE BASIC PRINCIPAL: from the very center point of all ideological projections there exists a village in which all talk, especially very complex talk of very complex things, is utterly worthless. When I looked at this small man looking at me I said, what are you looking at? And he said, "When I was twelve my mother gave birth to a glass box and in that glass box was my father, a very extremely holy man with long hair and a longlong beard bearing the color of bronze. And for years we clipped his hair and made baskets and furniture and clothing. But one day our father decided his days as a father and husband had come to an end, and he took off with a tribe of Buddhists into the Peruvian forest never to come out again. Supposedly they were meditating and dissolving into emptiness, but one night he came to me in a dream and told me what had really happened: They had gone to a local DSW shoe warehouse, bought some real-nice expensive-looking leather walking boots and moved to the largest city on earth where they walked up and down the sidewalks and onto and off of trains either a.) for the rest of eternity or b.) until they finally come to Yonge Street, the longest and most curvy street that has ever existed in all of time."

ONE NIGHT I DREAMT there was an extremely old man lying next to me in a tunnel of windows where a bird flew wall to wall. But when the old man asked me to describe the bird I couldn't, I just couldn't! And because we were in the underground tunnel of Fritz Perl's sub-sub-conscious, the old man, who was dressed like a tiger, said that perhaps this meant that the university was not the proper church for me after all and had I considered philanthropy as a profession. I said to this old tiger man that I wasn't in the market for a church, though once when I was at a poor distance from the stage I did try to get up closer to hear the great American band playing music. But I couldn't because there were fields of humans and also because of spiritualism, which is sort of like patriotism, but with less flair. Anyway, they all had these little black combs and were combing their hair like it was school picture day. And I chose the tie-dye background and wore a scrunchy in my hair and you, I said to the very old man, chose an American flag background and wore your hair parted in the middle with one ponytail on the left side of your head but no ponytail on the right side, and all the rest of your hair was down except for the one ponytail and oh! It looked so nice that I lent you my scrunchy because it was blue and matched the American flag background. And then I sat down because my heart ached soso much because I didn't have, nor have I ever had, a mutual fund. And so I sat and stared for a very long time into the frozenblueopalaxis of my future investments. And I said into the hovering ethers that no, a proper God has not yet been born. And all the while you were posing and smiling for the neon flash of the camera so nicely and I felt soso proud of you and your school pictures.

ON ANOTHER DAY, A SMALL MAN SAYS TO ME, he says, "When you walk into a room it is as if you are carrying the dead weight of a sea inside of you." And I says to him, "Sometimes it is as if I am carrying the weight of all seas of all time that ever existed." And this small man says to me, "Sometimes you look so light I wonder how it is you don't just float away." And then it was made clear that I would have to reveal to him my most recent DSM diagnosis, which involved being haunted by the ghosts of something like eight different Polish immigrants all at the same time. And so, because of this, I went out to the great precipice and I says to the Great Atmospheric Listener that, I hear a hundred birds circling my house and sometimes I think they are ghosts as well and what does the DSM have to say about this? Then a small man, overhearing this, got out his most recent version of the DSM to read my newest diagnosis, which involved a five year battle with a great and heavy tiredness and would I make it through? I wondered. The small man said he didn't know but that he would make me a nice feather blanket out of all these birds circling outside my house to keep me wrapped up very warm and comfortable for all those five years. And so, he took his shotgun and went outside and began shooting all the hundreds of birds and defeathering them and stuffing the feathers into a nice soft cotton fabric even though he was allergic to down.

I HAVE WRAPPED MYSELF in this very nice finch feather blanket and locked myself in a 99-cent birdcage because some priest wanted to cut me open but I wouldn't let him. I hate it when birds migrate, I tell this man, I hate it when the top most layer is not distinguished from realtrue air, and I hate it when some PhD comes strutting down the street in his high-holy top hat reciting passages from the DSM! I am awake, I say, but in my dreams I am putting on my father's socks and preparing various physical feats so the crowds will be impressed. Then this high-holy man comes strutting along telling me, "I may be able to give you another diagnosis that is more severe but that may reverse your previous diagnosis." And I said only if it involves a prescription for Valium. And he says, "Sure," and so off we go strutting down the long glass hall to his office, all the while with the ghosts in my hair shouting things like "mind fuck" and "fuck mind" and "Get on your best suit we're going to the local tavern to drink Kingfisher Beer." Then I just walked right out of a green door like a real-life architect into a sea of various high-class buildings and walked until I reached the slums, where I could finally be happy, like a real-life child in the actual museum of modern-day history.

AT THIS POINT, A MAN AND I have spread our many tears over the various ash piles of our dead pets. And while I sit eating the tiniest most small orange that has existed in all of time, this small man begins tracing lines into the air with his finger, then calculating the exact latitude and longitude of the intersection of the lines, so that he can shout them down to me inside my own personal darkness, and I can begin to weave a ladder from the braids of ghost hair and slowly climb my way out. Once out, I say to this small man, I will take you back to Kentucky in a covered wagon and, just as the North Wind begins to blow tiny fish skeletons all over the land, we will see that we have actually been looking through two layers of trifocals turned backwards this whole time, "And while you have been down inside your own personal darkness trying to weave a ladder out," a small man explains, "I have been knitting myself into my own sort of darkness. But let me just tell you this one thing: I think the laundry chute travels backwards through this apartment building and if you just slide down into it, it will be like a reverse puberty, but one that is like breaking through the tinfoil layer to get to the Valium and in an instant oh! If I could only find where I placed my plastic-footed-beaded jay-jay and put it on just one last time for old-times' sake and remember all the times when you played a militant in a black-and-white film and I played a real-life postman traveling though the tollbooths and over the hills of America, when really all each of us ever hoped for was to become classic Sears Catalogue underwear models. And look at us now, each at opposite ends of our own personal darknesses, weaving our ways toward one another. Except finally, once again, we can look up and see that all the little golden lemons are hanging over our genius heads."

NOTES

"For and After Federico García Lorca," borrows a few words and phrases from Federico García Lorca's *Poet In New York,* including: "moon of cancer," "broken microscopes," "crocodiles sleep," and "one must . . ."

My poem "This Is Agony" contains the phrase "strange sky," which was borrowed from Lorca's "Blind Panorama of New York."

My poem "What We Did With The Old Pins," was inspired by the line "I know the most secret use/for an old, rusted pin," in Lorca's poem "Double Poem Of Lake Eden."

My poem "What we did with the old pins," uses the phrases "deserted plaza," "pure holes," and "plaster" from Lorca's "Nocturne Of The Hole."

In Section 2, my line "I go into and out of this supermarket whenever I want," is a variation of a line from Inger Christensen's book *It,* her line being, "I go into and out of this paradise whenever I want."

In Sections I and 2, I use words gathered while reading Eric Baus's *The To Sound,* including: carp, draw circles, the shape of birds, sister's, doctor, dentist, x-ray, cathedral, cartographer, nitrogen, twenty blocks away, swoons, dousing, build me, aperture, transparent, and the phrase "If I say . . . I mean."

ACKNOWLEDGMENTS

Thank you Magic Mentor Jeff Friedman for your support and encouragement. Also, thanks (in memoriam) to Barbara Benoit.

Portions of this book were published in the chapbooks *the christ hairnet fish library* (Dancing Girl Press) and *A Small Man Looked At Me* (Little Red Leaves Press).

Thank you to the editors of the following journals for publishing poems from this work:

Anthem Journal: "We're at the actual museum" and "I am in the next room"

Bateau: "Last night I dreamt" and "All my life I've been dragging"

Boog City Review: "It will take me twenty paces"

Dear Sir: "I was out way out", "Heidegger was doing his feelings", "Heidegger touches my ocean", "If I were a wife", and "I'm alive in the tiny colony"

The New Orleans Review: "I'm tired of these sorts of walls", "As if a man splits", and "In the event that we are, after all"

Poetrycrush: "For and After Federico García Lorca", "A small man looked at me", and "I told this small man"

Poetry City U.S.A.: "This is Agony"

Scapegoat Review: "It will take me twenty paces", "I don't think I can take credit for this", and "What we did with the old pins"

Poems from this manuscript have also appeared in the anthology *Some Things Are True That Never Happened*: "They made blindfolds", "It's impossible to reach my tiny body", and "Take, for instance, a planet"

Sara Lefsyk has two previous chapbooks, *the christ
hairnet fish library* (Dancing Girl Press) and *A Small
Man Looked At Me* (Little Red Leaves Press). Her
work has appeared in such places as *Anthem Journal,
Bateau, Dear Sir, The Greensboro Review, The New Orleans
Review,* Phoebe and *Poetrycrush* among others. She
lives in Colorado where she is a baker, an assistant
editor at Trio House Press and a creator of various
items such as miniature handmade books.